MILITARY MACHINES

Jane A.C. West

Rising Stars UK Ltd.
22 Grafton Street, London W1S 4EX
www.risingstars-uk.com

nasen
Helping Everyone Achieve

NASEN House, 4/5 Amber Business Village, Amber Close, Amington, Tamworth, Staffordshire B77 4RP

Published 2008

Series Consultant: Lorraine Petersen
Cover design: Neil Straker Creative
Design: Clive Sutherland
Editorial: Frances Ridley
Illustrations: Bill Greenhead for Illustration Ltd
Photographs: Alamy: 10, 11, 17, 18-19, 20, 23, 24, 28
Corbis: 8, 26, 27, 28, 38
Eurofighter.com: 4, 11, 12, 13
Getty Images: 24, 26, 27, 29, 30, 32-33, 36, 39, 40, 42, 44, 45, 47
PA photos: 14-15
U.S Federal Government images: 23, 29, 34-35, 46

British Library Cataloguing in Publication Data.
A CIP record for this book is available from the British Library.

ISBN: 978-1-84680-448-9

Printed by: Craftprint International Ltd, Singapore

The publishers and author would like to thank the following for permission to use copyright material.
Eurofighter images © www.eurofighter.com with special thanks to Wolfdietrich Hoeveler.
The U.S. Federal Government

Dedicated to Sergeant Pen Farthing, 42 Commando, and the Nowzad Dogs.

Contents

MILITARY MACHINES: THE BIG PICTURE

Military machines are designed to do different jobs. Some machines carry troops to and from the battlefield. Other machines carry deadly weapons. Some military machines *are* deadly weapons.

Find the answers to these questions.

1. What is the EuroFighter's top speed?
2. What is a 'Battle Taxi'?
3. Why did Private Johnson Beharry win the V.C. medal?

ZOOMING IN ...

Remote control

Aircraft at sea

Hunter-killer submarine

Planes that travel faster than sound

Tanks you can live in

Troops on the move

War machines

106

FIGHTER PLANES

Fighter planes are designed to attack other aircraft. They have speed, strength and style. They carry a pilot and sometimes another crew member. They are smaller and lighter than bomber planes. Fighter planes can make fast and sudden twists, turns, rolls and dives.

Chapter 6

A DESIGN CLASSIC

Concorde was a passenger plane. It flew for the first time in 1969. It was the most stylish plane ever built. Concorde had delta wings. This means that they looked like triangles with the tips cut off. Concorde was sleek and fast. It could fly at **supersonic** speeds.

Concorde flew for the last time in 2003.

Concorde flying, showing triangular wing shape

The Eurofighter, showing triangular wing shape

The Eurofigher is a fighter plane. It has state-of-the-art **weapons systems** and carries bombs. Its first test flight was in 1994.

It has the same delta wing design as Concorde. Like Concorde, it can fly faster than the **speed of sound**.

Unlike Concorde, the EuroFighter uses the latest computer technology to fly. It performs fast turns and difficult moves that would make an ordinary passenger airsick!

The Typhoon EuroFighter

There are 43 Eurofighter Typhoons in the Royal Air Force fleet. The Typhoon's top speed is 1,320 mph – nearly twice the speed of sound. Each plane costs £61 million.

A Typhoon pilot uses computer screens instead of ordinary controls. The screens show:

- maps
- information about the plane
- information about the battle.

Eurofighters may be the last fighter planes that carry human pilots. In the future, the planes will be remote controlled.

FAST FACT

A typhoon is a very fast wind – like a hurricane.

31

TANKS

Tanks have wheels that run on tracks. They can move fast over rough ground. Tanks are used to stop enemies on foot. The main battle tank in the British Army is the FV4034 Challenger.

TRAINING DAY: PRIVATE WINSTON'S DIARY

Tuesday, 5th May

Today I was shown how to drive a Challenger 2. Fantastic!

The tank carries four soldiers – commander, gunner, weapons loader and driver. It's got six forward gears and two reverse gears – and it's fast. Its top speed is 45 mph.

The tank has a **boiling vessel** – so we can make tea! We get boil-in-the-bag meals in our **ration packs**. We can heat these up in the **BV**, too.

The tank also has a special life-support system. The crew could live inside the tank for days if a **nuclear bomb** or a **biological weapon** went off. There's even a toilet! But it's very dark inside the tank and there's not much room – I kept banging my head!

DR 39 AA

The Challenger 2

The Challenger 2 is made by a British company called Alvis Vickers. The tank is famous for its heavy **armour**. The armour stops bullets, fire and **shrapnel**.

In Iraq, a Challenger 2 was hit by 70 **RPG**s. The tank and its crew survived. The armour is so good that the government has made it 'top secret'.

CHALLENGER FACTS

- The gun turret spins round 360° in 9 seconds.
- The tank can pull over 50 tonnes and weighs 62.5 tonnes.
- Each tank costs £5.6 million.

09 EA 47

ARMOURED PERSONNEL CARRIERS (APCs)

APCs are armoured vehicles. They carry soldiers to and from battlefields. They can stop small bullets but not heavy fire. This makes them different from tanks. Some APCs have tracks and other APCs have wheels.

Tracks or wheels?

SOLDIER 1: Wheeled APCs are faster and lighter.

SOLDIER 2: But their armour is lighter, too. They can't take a direct hit by an RPG.

SOLDIER 1: A train has to take tracked APCs to the battlefield. That can take days or weeks. You can drive wheeled APCs there.

SOLDIER 2: It's easy to damage the rubber tyres on a wheeled APC.

SOLDIER 1: If you only damage one track on a tracked APC it can't move!

SOLDIER 2: Yes, but tracked APCs can go over rougher ground.

SOLDIER 3: The American Army uses Humvees. You can fit tracks over their wheels when the ground gets rough. In the future, you may be able to fit tracks on all wheeled APCs.

A Humvee with snow tracks fitted to its wheels

Troops on the move

The main job of an APC is to move troops. Soldiers call APCs 'Battle Taxis', or 'Battle Buses'. APCs can go across sand, rocks, mud, snow and ice. Many APCs can go across ponds and small lakes. Tracked APCs use their tracks to get across water. Wheeled APCs use **propellers** or water jets to give them extra power.

The British Army has 1,500 FV432 APCs. There are no gun holes in the FV432. The troops must get down on to the ground to fight.

The latest APCs have a special hull shape that 'pushes' bomb blasts away.

Ratel 90 with V-shaped hull

38309

CLOSE-UP: THE FIRST AND SECOND WORLD WARS

The First World War, 1914–1918

Fighter plane

RAF fighter plane, The Sopwith Camel, 1917

Planes were used for close combat fighting in the First World War.

Tank

British Army Mark IV Tank, 1918

Tanks used to be called ‘land ships’.

Battleship

British battleship, HMS Dreadnought, 1906-1919

The Dreadnought was the fastest battleship in the world.

Submarine

German U-boat, 1914-1918

German submarines sank 11 tonnes of shipping in the First World War.

The Second World War, 1939–1945

Fighter plane

The Supermarine Spitfire, RAF fighter plane, 1939

The wings of the Spitfire are shaped like a seagull.

Tank

World War 2, American M4 Sherman Tank, 1942-1955

50,000 of these tanks were made during the Second World War.

Battleship

German battleship, KMS Bismarck, 1941

This battleship was so dangerous that Royal Navy ships were told to: "Sink the Bismarck!"

Submarine

Imperial Japanese Navy, 400 class submarine, 1939-1945

The largest submarine of the Second World War.

SUBMARINES

Submarine boats operate under the sea. Hunter-killer submarines are designed to attack enemy ships. Some submarines can sail all the way around the world without rising to the surface. That's more than 25,000 miles!

Interview with a Submariner

Q: Tell us about the submarine you serve on.

A: It's nuclear powered. We could stay under the sea for years – we'd run out of food before we ran out of power.

Q: How do you get fresh air to breathe?

A: We don't. We have machines that get **oxygen** from the seawater.

Q: What do you like about your job?

A: I can travel around the world for free.

Q: What don't you like?

A: There's no privacy and not much room. Officers have their own rooms but the crew sleep in bunk beds. Also, I don't see my family for months at a time.

Q: What's your greatest fear?

A: Having a fire on board or water starting to leak in.

Virginia Class Submarine

The Virginia Class is an attack submarine. It carries 134 men. It also carries nuclear weapons. It is designed to find and destroy enemy submarines and ships.

The Virginia Class is powered by nuclear engines. Its top speed is 29 mph. It can dive 255 metres below the sea. Each of these subs costs $2 billion – about £1,000,000,000.

SUB FACT

Submarines used to have **periscopes** to see outside. The Virginia Class puts up two special masts, instead. The masts are fitted with cameras and laser **rangefinders**.

PROJ
30
9

AIRCRAFT CARRIERS

Aircraft carriers are warships that act as mini airbases. They carry helicopters and planes near to the war zone. This gives a country 'air power' even if the war is thousands of miles away.

WHAT AIRCRAFT?

Issue 128

Britain Needs More Air Power

A recent report says that Britain needs more air power. We asked a defence expert to explain:

'Our aircraft carriers only carry nine Harrier Jump Jets. We need aircraft carriers that will carry 40 to 50 planes and helicopters.

The report recommends that we get two big aircraft carriers. These will replace the three small aircraft carriers that we have at the moment.

The report recommends STOVL aircraft carriers.

Harrier jump jet

These carry planes that can take off and land in a very small space. The F-35 Lightning II would be ideal.

The report also recommends petrol engines because nuclear engines are too expensive. However, the carriers must be able to sail over 18,000 km without refuelling.'

Two new aircraft carriers

The British government has ordered two new aircraft carriers. Each ship will carry 48 aircraft or 25 Chinook helicopters. The ships are so big that they won't fit in any British docks. New docks will have to be built for them.

The new aircraft carriers will be even larger than this one.

The two carriers will cost £1.4 billion each. The HMS *Queen Elizabeth* will be finished in 2014. The HMS *Prince of Wales* will be finished in 2016.

CARRIER FACTS

- Weight – 75,000 tonnes
- Length – 274 metres
- Crew – 600 sailors.

MACHINES AND MEN

At the start of World War One soldiers still went to war on foot or on horseback. Since then, military machines have become bigger, faster and safer. But war is still dangerous for a soldier – they put their lives at risk.

A Brave Man

Private Johnson Beharry was driving a 30 tonne Warrior tank in Iraq in 2004. Suddenly, the Warrior was attacked with RPGs and bullets and filled with smoke.

Private Beharry knew he had to keep driving or he and the other soldiers would die. He drove with the hatch open so that he could see. Then he was wounded in the head. Blood got into his eyes and made it hard to see – but he kept on driving.

He said:

"Maybe I was brave, I don't know. I think anyone else could do the same thing."

Private Beharry was badly hurt but he saved the lives of his fellow soldiers. He was given the **VC** medal for his bravery.

Computers take control

The latest fighter planes and bombers have human pilots. But in the future, planes and other machines will be operated by **remote control**. Some of these machines are already in use.

The ScanEagle is a spy plane without a pilot. It is about the size of a model plane. It is launched using a catapault. A camera sends back photos of the places it flies over.

A remote controlled TALON robot. This robot is used for bomb disposal.

In the future, fewer soldiers may be needed. But these soldiers will have to be even more highly trained. They will have to operate very complex machines.

GLOSSARY

Armour	protects vehicles or people
Biological weapon	killing people with deadly germs (also called germ warfare)
Boiling vessel (BV)	a kettle
Nuclear bombs	bombs that use nuclear power
Oxygen	a gas
Periscope	viewing tube on a submarine
Propeller	curved blades that 'push' through water or air
Rangefinder	measures distance from weapon to target
Ration packs	army food
Remote control	controlled from a distance – for example, by a computer
RPG	stands for Rocket Propelled Grenade
Shrapnel	pieces of metal from an exploded bomb
Speed of sound	700 miles per hour
Supersonic	faster than the speed of sound
STOVL	Short Take Off and Vertical Landing
VC	Victoria Cross medal
Weapons systems	computers that control guns and bombs

INDEX